S.S. 192.]

O.B./1432/A.
40/W.O./5715

THE EMPLOYMENT OF MACHINE GUNS.

PART I.
TACTICAL

(ISSUED

T0326016

January, 1918.

(B 13688) Wt. w.4855 – PP 805 18M 2 18 H&S

FireStep
Editions

www.firesteppublishing.com

FireStep Publishing
Gemini House
136-140 Old Shoreham Road
Brighton
BN3 7BD

www.firesteppublishing.com

First published by the General Staff, War Office 1918.
First published in this format by FireStep Editions,
an imprint of FireStep Publishing, in association with
the National Army Museum, 2013.

NATIONAL
ARMY
MUSEUM

www.nam.ac.uk

ISBN 978-1-908487-62-9

Cover design FireStep Publishing
Typeset by FireStep Publishing
Printed and bound in Great Britain

Please note: *In producing in facsimile from original historical documents, any
imperfections may be reproduced and the quality may be lower than modern
typesetting or cartographic standards.*

CONTENTS.

PART I.

CONTENTS—*continued.*

NOTE.—*This manual has been drawn up mainly for the use of the British Armies in France. It is intended to serve also as a guide for Expeditionary Forces in other theatres of war.*

INDEX.

PART I.

A.

S.

T.

V.

W.

THE EMPLOYMENT OF MACHINE GUNS.

INTRODUCTION.

1. Recent experience has rendered necessary a revision of former instructions on the subject of the employment of Machine Guns.

2. Next to the Artillery, the Machine Gun is the most effective weapon employed in modern war, and against troops in the open at suitable ranges it is proportionately even more effective than Artillery, for the fire of one Machine Gun is more annihilating than that of one Gun or Howitzer.

It is therefore essential to success that the problems of Machine Gunnery should be appreciated and studied not only by Machine Gunners, but also by all those who have in their hands the organization and direction of Machine Gun work.

3. Unless the personnel of the Machine Gun Corps, both officers and men, understand thoroughly the branch of the Army which they will be called upon closely to support, co-operation becomes weak. Machine Gun officers, therefore, will receive instruction in Cavalry or Infantry tactics and organization at Army or Corps Schools, or by attachment to Regiments or Battalions.

The technical properties of Machine Guns with a steady firing platform enable use to be made of indirect fire, and accuracy to be maintained at long ranges. If full value is to be obtained from these powers, the personnel of the Machine Gun Corps must adapt the methods employed by the Field Artillery, in so far as they are suitable for Machine Guns, and reach a high standard of scientific knowledge. Every opportunity should therefore be taken of attaching Machine Gun officers to Field Artillery Batteries for periods of instruction.

4. The study of Machine Guns and their employment may be divided into three parts:—

> (a) The technical properties of the Machine Gun, including its mechanism.
>
> This part is covered by the " Handbook of the .303-in. Vickers Machine Gun."

(b) The tactical employment of Machine Guns.

This is dealt with in Part I. of the present publication. The matter contained in it is by its nature less specialized than that contained in (c): but it is impossible for the student to handle practically the problems of Machine Gun tactics, if he does not possess sufficient technical knowledge to appreciate the powers and limitations of the weapon, the basis on which the fire of one or more guns is directed, and the conditions under which in any particular situation the fullest fire effect will be obtained. Parts I. and II. must, therefore, be studied in conjunction.

(c) The organization and direction of Machine Gun fire, including the theoretical considerations affecting the fire power of the Machine Gun, a thorough understanding of maps and the instruments and appliances used in Machine Gunnery, and the practical application of Machine Gun fire to meet all tactical requirements.

This comprises Part II. of the present publication.

5. The distinguishing feature of modern Machine Gunnery is its offensive power. The offensive intention has always been present, but lack of training and technical equipment hindered its realization and led to the impression that the Machine Gun, whilst a powerful weapon in the defence of ground gained, could do little to assist the attacking troops in its capture.

Modern Machine Gunnery has reversed this passive tendency, and recent experience proves that the methods of offence now employed by Machine Gunners are viewed with confidence by the troops for whose support they have been designed. Therefore in future the Machine Gun must be regarded not merely as a defensive weapon, but as a weapon capable of supporting troops during an attack and protecting them against counter-attack during and after consolidation. In every operation Machine Guns must be organized, and their fire directed, with a view to developing to the full their offensive power; and in all training the offensive spirit in Machine Gunnery must be inculcated.

NOTE.—The terms "Machine Gun," "Barrage," and "Battery" are used throughout the present publication in the following senses:—

Machine Gun, to denote the 303 Vickers Machine Gun.

Barrage fire by Machine Guns is the fire of a large number of guns acting under a centralized control, directed on to definite lines or areas, in which the frontage engaged by a gun approximates 40 yards. (*See* Part II., Sec. 17, para. 1.)

Battery.—A battery of Machine Guns only exists as a tactical unit in the Motor Machine Gun Branch of the Machine Gun Corps. In the Cavalry and Infantry Branches the word is merely used as being the most convenient term for denoting a suitable number of Machine Guns placed under an officer as a fire unit for a particular purpose. (*See* Part I., Sec. 6.)

PART I.—TACTICAL EMPLOYMENT.

CHAPTER I.

1.—GENERAL CONSIDERATIONS.

1. The task which Machine Guns are called upon to perform may be divided, to speak generally, into two:—

(*a*) The direct support of Infantry Battalions by means of direct or indirect fire to enable them to advance in the attack or to assist them to maintain their position in the defence.

(*b*) The indirect support of Infantry Battalions by means of neutralizing or harassing fire, by which the fighting efficiency of the enemy is reduced.

2. The means adopted in fulfilment of this task may be summarised as follows:—

(*a*) In warfare of highly organized defences:—

Creeping or standing barrages, frontal or enfilade, in co-operation with the Artillery to cover the Infantry advance, and direct fire and defensive barrages to support the Infantry Battalions when they have gained their objectives.

Neutralizing fire, *i.e.*, intense searching fire on areas from which long-range Rifle and Machine Gun fire can be brought to bear against our troops.

Harassing fire.

Barrage fire to cover raids.

Direct fire and defensive barrages for the repulse of attacks initiated by the enemy.

(*b*) In warfare of improvised defences and in open fighting:—

Offensive and defensive tasks of the same nature, including tasks that have hitherto been allotted almost entirely to the Field Artillery, but for which there may not be sufficient Artillery available.

Against an enemy in shell-hole defences or in the open, searching fire will be effective at distant ranges (2,500—3,000 yards).

3. Accurate indirect fire is necessary in most of the above work, and, therefore, Machine Gun officers must be trained to organize Machine Guns for collective action in support of Infantry Battalions, both by indirect fire and by direct fire wherever this is possible.

4. When employed on the defensive the Machine Gun is a great economiser of men, for owing to its fire power it enables a defended line or area to be held by a minimum of rifles, thereby enabling the mass of the Infantry to be kept further back, ready for counter-attack or a subsequent offensive.

In particular, the fire power of the Machine Gun enables : —

> (a) The ground gained in an offensive to be held by the minimum of men, thereby reducing the casualties from subsequent bombardment, though it must be borne in mind that if a Machine Gun be destroyed, a big gap may be created.

> (b) A minimum of men, compatible with keeping the trench system in repair, to be kept in the line in ordinary trench warfare, thereby lessening the daily wastage from casualties and trench sickness, and the loss of efficiency through long periods of trench life.

> (c) The enemy to be held on one portion of the battle front with the minimum of Infantry and Artillery, while the maximum of Infantry and Artillery are concentrated for offensive action on another portion of the front, where decisive action is intended.

CHAPTER II.

WARFARE OF HIGHLY ORGANIZED DEFENCES— THE OFFENSIVE.

2.—PRINCIPLES OF THE ATTACK.

1. The Machine Guns available for any operation are most effectively employed when they are organized as a whole in accordance with a general plan, and allotted to formations in accordance with the tactical requirements of the situation. Machine Gun resources must be kept fluid, the work of every gun considered and a definite *rôle* allotted to it.

2. There must be co-ordination of the Machine Gun work throughout the whole force taking part in any operation. In a big operation the Machine Gun barrage work will form part of the Corps plan, and will be co-ordinated with that of the Corps on the flanks.

3. Direct fire over the sights at the target is the most effective form of Machine Gun fire. But although frequent opportunities should be forthcoming for employing with effect the direct fire of Machine Guns in open fighting in the attack as well as in the defence, the opportunities for using this form of fire to support Infantry in the attack of highly-organized defences are less numerous.

4. The offensive power of the Machine Gun has been increased by the progress made in the tactical employment of large numbers of Machine Guns for indirect fire. The experience of recent fighting proves that in attacks on organized and improvised defences alike, Machine Guns have rendered most assistance to the Infantry when they have been handled collectively and used in the main to give indirect fire, and that to resist counter-attacks the fullest value from Machine Guns is obtained by a combination of direct and indirect fire, part of the guns being retained in the rear to put down an overhead barrage on an S.O.S. line, and part being sent forward to support closely the attacking Infantry.

5. It must be remembered that while the Machine Guns always fight with Infantry Battalions, they do not necessarily fight from the same positions.

3.—CLASSES OF GUNS.

The Machine Guns available for an operation will be divided into two classes:—

      (*a*) Forward Guns, that is, the guns allotted to Infantry Brigades to go forward in support of the attacking Battalions, and carry out consolidation in depth of the ground won. These guns are definitely under the control of the Brigade Commander.

      (*b*) Rear Guns, that is, the guns which supply barrage and other forms of covering fire from positions in rear.

In addition, the question of holding some guns in reserve should always be considered, both by Divisional and by Brigade Commanders.

4.—ROLE OF FORWARD GUNS.

1. The *rôle* of every gun will be laid down in orders, namely, the location at zero, the route of advance, the final locality from which it is to be employed, the nature of that employment, and the Report Centres through which orders will reach the commanders of Forward Guns.

The use of aeroplane photographs, both vertical and oblique, are of great assistance in selecting routes, forward dumps, etc.

2. Apart from exceptional circumstances, such as when they form part of a detached force, these guns should not be definitely attached to Infantry Battalions.

The Machine Gun is not a suitable weapon to send forward tied to an Infantry Battalion, for the following reasons:—

      (*a*) Its weight, which makes it practically impossible for the Machine Gunner to keep up with the Battalion. Even if he succeeds in doing so, he becomes too exhausted to be useful until some time has elapsed.

      (*b*) Its visibility, as compared with the Lewis Gun, which makes it difficult at short notice to find a concealed fire position.

      (*c*) Now that the Infantry Battalion has a large number of Lewis Guns, the necessity for attaching Machine Guns to it has ceased to exist. The Lewis Gun and other Battalion weapons are usually sufficient for repelling early local counter-attacks. Machine Guns should aim at getting into their defence positions in time for the " setpiece " counter-attacks which come later.

3. Too many Machine Guns should not be pushed forward into the advanced portions of the captured position for early organization for defence, as this only results in useless loss of personnel and material, and in reducing the number of guns available for the S.O.S. barrage by which the Infantry are protected during organization.

4. The guns will usually work in sub-sections of two guns, each sub-section being under an officer.

5. The location of the guns at Zero will be chosen with regard to the line on which the hostile barrage will most probably first descend. They should as a rule do no firing before their advance. Thus they will be packed up and their personnel fresh when the time to move forward arrives. An exception to this would be guns taking part in a barrage during the earlier phases of an attack and being picked up by troops passing through to take part in a later phase of the operations.

6. In order that they may not become mixed in the *melée,* they will not follow the attacking waves too closely. The advance will be by " bounds " along previously selected routes. The halting place at the end of each " bound " will be given in advance, and should not be in proximity to any prominent landmark.

7. The localities from which the guns are to be employed finally will be laid down in orders, and representatives of the Forward Guns, preceded by their Scouts, will reconnoitre these localities and choose the actual position of each gun.

8. There are two ways of conducting this reconnaissance, by :—

(*a*) Each " bound " being reconnoitred separately.

(*b*) Representatives going forward with the Infantry to the final localities, and sending back for the guns when they are required.

9. It is usually best to cross No Man's Land early, so as to avoid the enemy barrage, and to make the enemy front or support lines the first halt. The guns will not leave the last halt to move forward to their final localities until the final position for each gun has been selected. They will then be guided direct to the positions from which they will come into action.

10. Open emplacements should, when possible, be prepared for them, before they are brought up.

11. The guns, both in their intermediate and final locations, will be distributed in depth.

12. Each sub-section of Forward Guns will be allotted a Report Centre, which normally will be the Headquarters of the Battalion in whose area they are operating. The commander of the sub-section will have runners at his Report Centre, so that messages can reach him, if he is not there himself at the time. The sub-section commander will report to the Battalion Commander in whose area he is operating, when his guns have taken up their allotted positions.

13. The Forward Machine Guns allotted to the consolidation will devote all their energy to the organization of their defensive positions, and in principle will not engage unimportant scattered parties of the enemy, or fire on hostile aircraft.

14. When the ground is favourable, "*Batteries of opportunity,*" consisting of not more than four Machine Guns* under the command of an officer, will move forward so as to reach points from which good forward observation is obtainable, early after the capture of the final objective.

15. The object of these Batteries is to seize every opportunity of inflicting loss on the enemy. They will:—

(a) Give close support by direct fire to the infantry during counter-attacks.

(b) Supplement and stiffen the system of defence of the area newly captured.

(c) Engage hostile artillery or bodies of troops within range.

(d) Engage hostile planes flying low.

16. The Batteries of opportunity must be handled with great boldness, and the largest initiative must be left to the Commanders regarding the selection of their position and the method of carrying out their task.

17. More than two Batteries of opportunity for a Division will seldom be required; the sector of activity of each Battery so employed will be allotted by the Division, and when more than a Division is engaged the employment of these Batteries will be co-ordinated by the Corps.

18. The Batteries of opportunity will inform the nearest Infantry Commander of their whereabouts, and will, when possible, work in co-operation with the nearest Artillery O.P.

---

* Experiments have proved that the fire of single Machine Guns at medium or long range is too scattered to be effective, and that the fire unit for long and medium range must consist of four Machine Guns.

5.—ROLE OF REAR GUNS.

1. The object of barrage fire by Machine Guns is two-fold: to assist the Infantry during an advance and to protect them during the organization of the captured position.

During an advance Machine Gun fire should be applied continuously either along the whole front under attack or on areas selected in advance by the General Staff. In the storm of a battle it is impossible to engage in detail the enemy targets ahead of the advancing line, and therefore it is necessary to sweep systematically all ground which may contain these targets. Similarly, after a successful advance, when the assaulting troops are in unfamiliar surroundings, ignorant of the exact disposition of their resources, and exhausted by the physical and nervous strain of their recent effort, and when organization of the captured position is not sufficiently advanced to be of great value in repelling a counter-attack, the Infantry's power of resistance must be strengthened by fire from the rear, which is applied the moment it is called for and on as wide a front as the counter-attack demands.

2. The Infantry advance will be covered by:—

(*a*) Standing barrages, placed on or beyond the various objectives to be attacked, and remaining there until such time as the Infantry advance renders it necessary for them to be placed further forward: or

(*b*) Creeping barrages, moving in front of the 18-pdr. creeping barrage and intensifying its effect; the Machine Gun lifts being not less than 100 yards. This is the more thorough method and, when time and resources permit, the more effective.

The covering barrages will, where necessary, be supplemented by, or may, on occasions (the controlling factor being the density of the artillery barrage), take the form of :—

(*a*) Standing barrages, placed on enemy lines of communication, likely approaches for enemy counter-attacks, and open ground over which the enemy must retire or be reinforced.

(*b*) Neutralizing fire, placed on commanding ground, or other areas from which observation can be obtained and fire directed by the enemy on our Infantry.

(*c*) Neutralizing fire, placed on positions which, though not being directly attacked at the time, are being enveloped or are holding up an attack already in progress.

3. During organization for defence the troops will be protected by S.O.S. barrages, arranged to go down as close in front of the line which is being organized as is consistent with the safety of the troops occupying it.

4. The direction from which barrage fire can be applied is either frontal, flanking or enfilade, but as enfilade fire is a form of flanking fire, it is only necessary to compare frontal with flanking barrages.

FRONTAL BARRAGE: —

Advantages :—It is usually the only one possible to employ on a general scale for covering the attacking troops in a big operation ; it gives a greater depth of beaten zone ; that is to say, the attacker walks up the cone instead of across it ; it is simple to arrange and carry out.

Disadvantages :—It requires more guns to cover a given front ; it cannot be placed so close to the attacking troops.

FLANKING BARRAGE:—

Advantages :—It can be placed rather closer to the Infantry ; it requires fewer guns to cover a given front ; it is more effective against trenches and streets which run at right angles to the general line of advance ; it is especially suitable for the protection of an exposed flank.

Disadvantages :—It is seldom possible, except in small operations, or in operations where one portion of the line is in advance of that from which the attack is being made ; it gives a narrower beaten zone, and is therefore more quickly traversed by the attacker ; it is more difficult to arrange and carry out.

It can therefore be concluded that the frontal barrage will be the normal type of barrage for covering the advance of the Infantry and forming the S.O.S. barrage line ; but that, when sufficient guns are available and the conformation of the line permits, a combination of frontal and flanking barrages will be the surest means of obtaining the fullest effect from the fire of Machine Guns.

5. When the ground is exceptionally favourable or has buildings on it, it is sometimes possible to use direct fire for covering the advance of troops. As a rule, however, if much Artillery is being employed, the dust renders observation impossible. Attacks frequently take place in the half-light of

early dawn, namely, at an hour when, owing to darkness or morning mist, it is not possible to see over the sights, and the control of a large number of guns by any means except that of the time-table is out of the question.

6. The Rear Guns, especially those forming the S.O.S. barrage line, form a strong rear line of defence in the event of the enemy breaking through, and at the same time a protection to our own Artillery and a reserve of power available to meet any new situation that may arise.

6.—ORGANIZATION OF REAR GUNS.

1. In a big operation the general plan will be drawn up by the Corps, in order that all the available Machine Guns may be used in the most effective manner and that the necessary co-operation with neighbouring Divisions and Corps may be assured. The same care must be taken to co-ordinate the Machine Gun barrages on neighbouring fronts as is taken with the Artillery barrages. The creeping barrage of the Machine Guns should be simple, and complicated lifts and changes of direction avoided.

2. The general plan having been drawn up and the Divisional Machine Gun Commanders conferred with, they in their turn will organize the guns at their disposal in accordance with that plan.

3. At the Divisional Conference the Divisional Commander, in consultation with the Brigade Commanders and the Divisional Machine Gun Commander, will have decided on the number of guns to be allotted to each category, and on the proportion of guns and personnel to be kept in reserve to replace casualties and to carry out reliefs.

4. The Rear Guns will be divided into Groups, usually one Group to each Brigade front. This will facilitate communication and ensure the Commander of a Group being in close touch with the Commander of the Brigade which he is supporting. Each Group will be sub-divided into " Batteries."* If the number of Batteries in any one Group exceeds four, it may be convenient for the sake of control to form sub-groups. The normal number of guns in a Battery is eight; it may be less, *i.e.*, four or six, but owing to difficulties of control should not be more.

---

* *See* note at end of Introduction.

5. Each Group will be under the command of an officer appointed as " Group Commander." It is essential that he should have his Headquarters at the Headquarters of the Brigade whose area his Group is covering.

He will be in telephonic communication with his Batteries, and will arrange for this communication to be duplicated by visual signalling whenever possible.

6. Each Battery will be under the command of an officer appointed as " Battery Commander."

7. In each Battery there should be at least one officer to four guns, and one N.C.O. not below the rank of Corporal to two guns. The Battery Commander is responsible that proper control is exercised throughout his Battery.

8. The Divisional Machine Gun Commander will be in close touch with Divisional Headquarters. He will be in communication with his Group Commanders, and also with the officer on the Corps Staff who is co-ordinating the operations of the Machine Guns.

7.—ORGANIZATION OF FORWARD AND REAR GUNS IN A DIVISION.

1. The tasks of the Forward Guns will be allotted by the Brigade Commander according to the tactical requirements.

2. If it is desired to increase the number of Rear Guns, it is sometimes possible to arrange that the formations which go through to the further objectives shall lend guns for barrage work during the earlier phases of the operation, and pick them up as they pass through, provided always that the combination of tasks does not render the personnel unfit for energetic action in their final forward position.

3. As a general rule, each Rear Gun will be allotted a frontage of 40 yards per gun with a closer concentration on points which require special attention.

8.—HARASSING FIRE.

1. The object of harassing fire is to prevent overland movement by the enemy and to dislocate the supply and maintenance of his front system. The fire will usually be at night. An organized scheme for carrying it out will be put in operation a certain number of days before an attack, and maintained in intensity until Zero day.

2. The original plan and the daily programme will be submitted to the Divisional Commander by the Divisional Machine Gun Commander, in co-operation with the Divisional Artillery Staff, and will be co-ordinated by the Corps. In order to secure a proper division of work, the Machine Gun plan of harassing fire should be part of a general scheme embracing the operations of Artillery, Machine Guns and Trench Mortars. Co-operation with the Intelligence (G.S.O.3) will ensure that the harassing scheme is kept up to date as regards " nerve centres " in the enemy's lines.

3. Key maps should be issued to Machine Gun Officers in charge of guns engaged in harassing fire. This reduces greatly the delay in getting out the daily fire programme.

4. For details of target and types of fire *see* Part II.

9.—SITING OF REAR GUNS.

1. Guns must be carefully sited in inconspicuous places. When the positions are in view of the enemy, the emplacements must be dug by night and kept camouflaged during the day. If the terrain is very exposed it may be inadvisable to dig any emplacements before Zero night, the ground being merely pegged out in advance. For specimens of emplacements used in recent offensive operations *see* Appendix II.

2. Care must be taken to avoid movement near the Battery positions by day, and the making of beaten tracks leading up to them, tracks being very visible on aeroplane photographs.

3. Once the battle has begun, it is often no longer possible, except in very favourable conditions, to conceal the Battery positions, and the success of the battle must be relied on to prevent the enemy being able to divert sufficient Artillery from his original programme to deal effectively with the Rear Guns.

4. Precautions should be taken against low flying aeroplanes. Machine Gun detachments are responsible for their own protection, but Lewis Guns, posted away from the Battery positions but within range of such aircraft, would prove valuable for protecting Rear Guns during the battle, if available.

10.—FORWARD MOVEMENT OF BATTERIES.

1. The arrangements for the forward movement of a large number of Batteries, with the necessary ammunition, spare parts, water, oil, etc., are complicated; and Divisional Machine

Gun Commanders are responsible for preparing the detailed instructions for the forward moves of the Batteries forming the Groups under their command.

2. Time of starting, route, halting places, final location, will be given to each Battery, and maps prepared showing all details.

In addition, the calculations necessary to enable the Batteries to open fire from their new positions in the shortest possible time will be worked out beforehand, and the necessary fire orders and fire organization tables issued. Oblique aeroplane photographs should be supplied to all Batteries moving forward.

3. Wherever possible pack animals should be used to assist the Batteries in their forward move. It may sometimes be advisable to place the pack animals, while they are waiting for the time to advance, in pits which have been dug in rear of the Battery, but not so close as to disclose its position.

4. Whether pack animals are used or not, Batteries require assistance from the Infantry on the scale of two extra carriers per gun. These must be picked men, selected for their physical strength and staying power, and they should be attached to the Machine Gun Companies for some time beforehand in order that they may be trained in their duties.

5. All forward moves should be rehearsed beforehand over ground which resembles as nearly as possible that actually to be crossed.

During these practices and at other times the personnel will be trained in the carrying of their loads for long distances, and everything possible will be done to increase their fitness for the task that they will have to perform.

11.—FINAL S.O.S. BARRAGE.

1. This should be arranged so as to provide a complete belt of fire along the whole front of the operation.

If the operation is one in which the length of the advance makes it necessary for the Artillery, or at any rate a portion of the Artillery, to move forward, it is all the more essential to provide this belt of Machine Gun fire as early as possible after the attacking troops have reached their final objective.

2. All necessary arrangements and calculations will be made beforehand (*see* Sec. 10, para 2).

3. These arrangements will contemplate the possibility of the attacking troops making good their final objective on one part of the front and failing to attain it on another. In order that the successful troops may not be compelled to withdraw, the protective barrage will have to be maintained ahead of them and at the same time drawn in to cover their exposed flank and the front of the troops who have advanced less far. This is only possible if and when the position of friendly troops is exactly known.

12.—UNITY OF METHOD IN ATTACK AND DEFENCE.

The method by which barrage fire is carried out is given in detail in Part II., and it is similar both for the attack and the defence, the only difference being that in defensive conditions the arrangements will on the whole be simpler. This unity of method is in accord with the fundamental unity between the offensive and defensive *rôles* of the Machine Gun. The attack, as already shown, implies the covering of an assault and the repulse of counter-attacks, and the defence, as will be shown in the sections which follow, develops an active nature in proportion as it is organized on scientific lines.

CHAPTER III.

WARFARE OF HIGHLY ORGANIZED DEFENCES— THE DEFENSIVE.*

13.—PRINCIPLES OF DEFENCE.

1. The plan of defence in normal trench warfare legislates for an area organized in depth by one or more defensive systems.

2. The Front System is composed usually of an elaborate network of trenches and strong points, arranged roughly in three lines, as follows:—

(*a*) A First Line, which is in the nature of an observation or outpost line, and which as a general rule comprises a series of posts held by small numbers of Infantry with the help of Lewis Guns; these posts being connected by trenches.

(*b*) A Second or Support Line, which consists of a continuous line held in strength by the Infantry.

(*c*) A Reserve Line, generally the Main Line of Resistance, which consists of a connected series of strong points designed to:—

(i.) Break up an enemy attack by denying to him the most important features.

(ii.) Form rallying points behind which troops driven from the front two lines can be reformed.

(iii.) Split up an enemy attack in such a way that hostile elements which break through between the points shall be exposed to destruction in detail.

(iv.) Allow of counter-attacks issuing between them for the purpose of ejecting from the two first lines an enemy who has succeeded in establishing himself in them.

3. Behind this Front System will be other defended lines, or systems, consisting of woods and villages prepared for defence, and of trenches and redoubts commanding features of tactical importance.

---

* To be read in conjunction with S.S. 196 " Trench Warfare Diagrams for Infantry Officers."

4. The methods of employing Machine Guns for assisting in the defence of the Front System will alone be considered in this publication. All the principles of Machine Gun defence are contained therein, and the extent to which the Rear Systems can at any time be manned depends on the guns and personnel available.

5. The principle of economy of force is that as few men as possible shall be employed in a purely defensive *rôle*, whilst as many as possible are kept ready for offensive action.

This principle is observed when the fire power of Machine Guns is so employed that the trench system is held by a minimum of rifles and consequently with a minimum wastage of man power. (*See* Sec. 1, para. 4.)

6. The fullest service, however, cannot be rendered to Infantry Battalions unless there is close co-operation between the Artillery and Machine Guns. This point has already been noticed in Section 8 in connection with Harassing Fire previous to an attack. In defence it is of no less importance. The defence provided by the Artillery, Machine Guns and Trench Mortars must be a combined scheme in which the several arms supplement one another. In places where, and on occasions when, the number of Field Guns available precludes a complete defensive barrage of Artillery fire, co-ordination is all the more important.

7. In case of an enemy attack the *rôle* of the Machine Guns is:—

> (*a*) To disorganize the attack in its origin by firing on the area from which it is launched.

> (*b*) Should the enemy penetrate into the defended area, to arrest him by annihilating fire at short ranges, and hold him up at all costs until time has been gained for the preparation and launching of a counter-attack.

8. This *rôle* necessitates arrangements whereby effective belts of Machine Gun fire can be placed in the path of an advancing enemy.

The aim is not to site Machine Guns so that every yard of ground is swept by Machine Gun Fire, but so to combine the Machine Gun defence with that of the Lewis Guns of Infantry Battalions, that Machine Guns will play the part dictated by the characteristics of the weapon and will not be wasted in doing work which can be performed by Lewis Guns, such as firing on small depressions or down trenches. Machine Gun fire should be reserved for protection on a bigger scale, covering the more important features and denying to the enemy the most favourable routes of advance. Points of tactical importance must be strongly covered even though, owing to a shortage of guns, it is necessary to leave gaps on parts of the front where an enemy attack is improbable.

14.—TYPES OF MACHINE GUN FIRE.

Belts of Machine Gun Fire are of different types, according to the way they are produced:—

Type A.

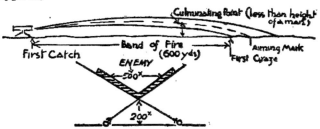

By bands of fire at short ranges where the culminating point is less than the height of a man. This kind of belt is especially suitable on flat ground, and it is very deadly; but, if used to cover the Front Line, it necessitates guns being placed well forward in the Front System.

Type B.

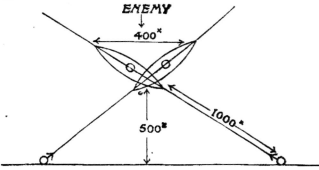

By oblique locking of beaten zones at moderate ranges.— This type covers less ground per gun, but it allows of guns being placed further back. The extent of the zone varies with the slope of the ground swept, being greater on ground falling with respect to the line of sight.

Type C.

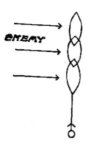

By locking in depth, that is to say, a flanking barrage. This is a practical application of combined sights. It is most suited for the protection of a salient or exposed flank, and it may be possible to apply it to a re-entrant when the guns themselves can be brought into a salient and fired almost parallel to the front. The width of the beaten zone of a Machine Gun being narrow, it may be advisable to duplicate this belt where a high degree of protection is required.

Type D.

By frontal fire, in which the front covered by each gun depends on the number of guns available, but should not be more than 50 yards. The efficacy of this type of belt depends on :—

> (i.) The number of guns available and their rate of fire.
>
> (ii.) The angle of dive of the bullets (angle of dive = angle of descent for range, that is, angle of ground+ angle of sight).
>
> (iii.) The time taken by hostile troops in passing through the belt.

This is the normal type of S.O.S. protective belt fired over the heads of the Infantry.

15.—DIRECT LAYING AND INDIRECT FIRE.

In comparing the scope for direct and indirect fire, it should be borne in mind that it is often possible to lay the guns by direct observation, and, subsequently, necessary to fire them indirect, either because the enemy's attack comes at night or early dawn, or because visibility is obscured by the smoke and dust of the enemy's bombardment and by his smoke screens. (*See* Sec. 5, para. 5.) Guns laid to fire direct should always be equipped for firing indirect, should the need arise.

16.—MUTUAL CO-OPERATION.

1. However numerous the guns employed, the defence will never possess the maximum power of resistance unless a complete plan of co-operation between the Machine Guns employed in a defended area is arranged.

2. This complete co-operation cannot be achieved unless the main plan of defence is laid down by the Corps for its whole front. This is necessary to secure :—

> (*a*) The linking-up of the defence on the flanks of neighbouring Corps and Divisions.
>
> (*b*) A continuity of policy. Divisions often stay only a short time in a particular sector ; and unless a continuous policy is adhered to, the system of defence is always in a state of flux and much time and labour are wasted.

3. Conversely, the execution of that part of the plan allotted to a Division must be a Divisional affair. This is necessary to ensure continuity of policy and proper co-operation between the Machine Gun Companies concerned.

4. Mutual Co-operation therefore implies:—

(*a*) A plan of defence which is outlined by the Corps and co-ordinated by the Division under its Divisional Machine Gun Commander This secures central direction, the pooling of resources, and, as the result, the maximum of flexibility combined with the maximum of economy.

(*b*) A system that facilitates the use on a large scale of oblique fire. For example, an attack delivered in force on a narrow front may momentarily overwhelm the defences of a Brigade. Assistance should always be forthcoming from the Brigades on either flank, but this will rarely be obtained in time, unless it is arranged in advance in the Divisional plan.

Recent experience shows that co-operation on Divisional lines becomes imperative when the enemy launches a sudden offensive. It is therefore desirable to forestall this necessity by adopting, while conditions are normal, a scheme of Machine Gun defence which is flexible and amenable to control.

17.—CO-OPERATION WITH OTHER ARMS.

1. Divisional and Brigade Commanders must ensure that the plan of Machine Gun defence is in harmony with the distribution of the troops whom it is designed to protect, and Battalion Commanders must co-ordinate their Lewis Guns with this scheme and prevent overlapping or waste of fire power. There are cases where a Machine Gun can do rather more reliably the work which belongs to a Lewis Gun, but only at the expense of neglecting work which is essential to the general scheme of defence and which the Machine Gun alone can do.

2. Co-operation with the Artillery and Trench Mortars is required in order:—

(*a*) To work out a S.O.S. line of combined Artillery, Trench Mortar and Machine Gun fire in the proper proportions and of the desired depth.

(*b*) To co-operate in schemes of harassing fire at all times, and not merely on the eve of a big attack.

(*c*) To obtain information about the enemy. which the Artillery with its more elaborate system of observation has at its disposal.

3. Co-operation with the Engineers and Pioneer Companies is required in order:—

(a) That new wire may be sited in accordance with the plans of the Commander by representatives of the Machine Guns, Engineers and Infantry acting in concert. Machine Gun positions and wire should be sited simultaneously.

(b) That emplacements may be of the type required under the latest conditions, especially with regard to camouflage and tunnelling.

18.—METHOD OF HOLDING THE FRONT SYSTEM.
(*See* Sec. 13, para. 2.)

A sector of trenches should not be regarded as a mere series of successive defence lines to be held one after another, but as a single defended area the protection of which is laid out upon a definite plan, according to the nature of the ground.

The first question to consider in drawing up a plan of Machine Gun Defence for any sector of trenches is the Main Line of Resistance; that is, the line beyond which the enemy's attack must not penetrate. A decision on this point will decide the correct allotment of guns in depth.

It is possible for an intensive Artillery bombardment to destroy the Front and Support Lines, including any Machine Guns that may be in them, unless they are accommodated in deep dug-outs. If guns are kept in deep dug-outs in front trenches their chances of coming into action are small, since by the time they are mounted the enemy will be on top of them.

Machine Guns therefore will usually be placed in rear of the Support Line. The responsibility of holding the Front Line rests with Infantry Battalions and their Lewis Guns, assisted from the rear by Machine Guns.

19.—NUMBER OF GUNS IN FRONT SYSTEM.

The number of guns employed in the Front System will be determined by:—

(a) The total number of guns available.

(b) The nature of the ground and the tactical situation.

(c) The amount of cover that can be provided and the time that it will take to bring the guns into action.

(d) The arrangements for the relief of gun teams. These must be adequate and are especially important when heavy shelling, bad accommodation and severe weather have to be faced.

20.—CLASSES OF GUNS.

In conformity with the principle of defence in depth, provision must be made for a combination of direct and indirect fire; and, as in the offensive, the Machine Guns will fall naturally into two categories:—

(a) Forward Guns. (*See* Sec. 4.)

(b) Rear Guns. (*See* Sec. 5.)

21.—FORWARD GUNS.

1. These guns should, where possible, be arranged in pairs, each pair under the command of an Officer, or Sergeant. Each gun must have a N.C.O. as Gun Commander.

2. They should usually be placed in rear of the Second or Support Line, and between it and the Reserve Line.

3. They should be able to fire either by direct or indirect fire:—

(a) On to No Man's Land, bringing oblique or flanking fire in front of the posts which constitute our Front Line. This is usually achieved by laying the lines of fire so that they pass between the posts and cross in front of them; *i.e.*, by the locking of Beaten Zones, as described in Sec. 14, Type B.

(b) On the ground between the Front and Support Lines, putting Bands of Fire across it, as described in Sec. 14, Type A.

22.—GUNS IN OR NEAR THE FRONT LINE.

As stated in Sec. 21, para. 2, the Forward Guns should not normally be placed in front of the Support Line.

In exceptional cases, however, it may be desirable to place one or more Forward Guns in or near the Front Line, *e.g.*, where they can be defiladed from the enemy by rising ground, and are able from this vantage point to bring fire on important roads or trench junctions further down the line.

In all cases where guns are in or near the Front Line they must have local protection against surprise. A party of bombers and riflemen should always be at hand, and a bombing post established to prevent approach within bombing range of the gun positions. As Machine Gunners are trained to throw bombs, they should be provided with a small stock for use in an emergency.

23.—REAR GUNS.

1. These guns will usually be placed in the neighbourhood and in rear of the Reserve Line or Main Line of Resistance.

2. The ideal programme for these guns would be:—

(*a*) To provide a complete S.O.S. barrage line along the whole front; this line to be normally beyond the Artillery barrage line.

(*b*) In the event of a hostile penetration beyond the Support Line, to place Bands of Fire across the front of the strong points in the Reserve Line. These bands should be so arranged that the fire comes between the strong points and crosses in front of them. Where the number of guns does not permit the first part of the programme to be carried out completely, arrangements should be made in conjunction with the Artillery (*see* Sec. 17, para. 3), to put the S.O.S. barrage on selected parts of the front.

3. The Rear Guns will usually be the guns employed for covering raids and other special enterprises. They will constitute a mobile reserve which will be in readiness to cope with emergencies on a particular part of the Divisional front or on the front of the Divisions on either flank. The fact that they are not involved in the close defence of the Front Line will facilitate conference with the Artillery and their detachment for special tasks.

24.—NIGHT FIRING BY FORWARD AND REAR GUNS.

1. In normal times the bulk of Machine Gun firing will be done at night. The execution of night firing must never be allowed to become a mechanical and perfunctory performance. In this work it is possible, even when the general situation is quiet, to maintain the offensive spirit.

2. The targets must be well selected and the volume of fire sufficient. The requisite intensity of fire should be obtained by increasing the number of Machine Guns rather than by allotting bigger tasks to a restricted number. Both classes of guns, therefore, forward and barrage, will be employed.

3. Each night's firing should be part of a programme, which is based on the information obtained by the Divisional Machine Gun Commander from the latest intelligence and the night firing programme of the Artillery.

4. Provided that an alternative position is available in case of need, it will usually be safe, and always more convenient, for guns which have well equipped S.O.S. positions concealed from view to do their night firing from these. But guns whose S.O.S. position is exposed or very close to the Front Line must move elsewhere for night work. This night position must allow of fire on the S.O.S. Line.

5. The difference between normal night firing and the harassing fire carried out mainly at night time prior to a " set-piece " attack (*see* Sec. 8) is merely one of degree. The methods and organization are identical.

25.—DEFENCE IN DEPTH AND THE " OFFENSIVE " DEFENCE.

An observance of the principles laid down will result in a zone of Machine Gun defences organized in depth rather than a series of positions covering, and limited to, successive trench lines. The object of placing Machine Guns in depth is to secure fire in depth from the enemy's front system back to our own reserve lines; but the guns themselves should not be dotted indiscriminately over the zone, as they will then not be easy to control, and the organization therefore not flexible. Control and flexibility are essential to the " offensive " defence mentioned in Sec. 23, para. 3, and Sec. 24 above. For this kind of work and the " set-piece " offensive itself the Machine Guns must always be prepared. A system of passive defence is destructive of efficiency, and, furthermore, overlooks the important function of inspiring the troops with confidence.

26.—FIRE CONTROL OF THE FORWARD GUNS.
(*See* Section 21.)

1. Direct observation of the situation from the gun position and fire on previously arranged S.O.S. lines will, as a rule, be the only methods of control possible once the enemy attack has commenced.

2. In order that the guns may be able to fire as directed in Sec. 21, para. 3, there will be two prescribed lines of fire, of which the first will bring them on to No Man's Land as described in Sec. 21, 3 (*a*), while they can be switched without delay on to the second as described in Sec. 21, 3 (*b*). Fire will be opened on the latter, as soon as it is ascertained that the

enemy has penetrated beyond the First Line into the vicinity of the Support Line, and the situation as regards our own troops is sufficiently clear.

Until then fire will be maintained on the S.O.S. line, and the barrage thus formed, combined with that of the Rear Machine Guns, Artillery and Trench Mortars, should prevent the enemy being reinforced, and enable the Infantry Battalions to deal with those of the enemy's troops which have succeeded in entering the front position.

3. Precise instructions must be issued as to the fire of these Forward Guns, and their action and lines of fire in case of an attack explained in advance to the Infantry Battalions concerned.

4. In an entrenched position, the ability to repulse the enemy does not depend on the number of men in the trenches before the bombardment begins, but on the amount of fire that can be delivered against the enemy when his barrage lifts and his Infantry advances. If the trenches are thickly manned :—

(a) Heavy loss is caused by the bombardment.

(b) Difficulty is experienced by the Forward Machine Guns in bringing fire to bear on the enemy without hitting their own troops.

5. These disadvantages are reduced to a minimum, when the First and Support Lines are held lightly and arrangements exist whereby certain portions of the trench system in, and in front of, the Second Line are marked as being in the danger zone of Machine Gun fire from the moment the S.O.S. Signal goes up, as well as later when the Machine Guns are firing on their second lines of fire in the manner just described.

The routes which will be used for movement between the Front and Support Lines should be definitely laid down and known by the Machine Gunners.

Arrangements of this nature will enable the full power of the Machine Gun to be developed from the beginning of the attack and maintained throughout. Large areas of ground will be denied to the enemy, his attack will be kept " below ground," that is to say, confined to working up the trenches themselves, and the task left to Infantry Battalions of dealing with those of the enemy who have penetrated beyond the Front Line will be facilitated.

6. Thus, by careful arrangements, precise instructions and a thorough understanding between Infantry Battalions and Machine Gunners, it will be possible to ensure that confusion, delay in opening fire and risk to our own troops from the fire of Machine Guns are minimised, and Battalions will be able to rely on obtaining support from the Machine Guns from the outset of the enemy attack.

27.—FIRE CONTROL OF THE REAR GUNS.

In a similar manner the Rear Guns will primarily have two lines of fire :—

(*a*) On their S.O.S. line.

(*b*) On their close defence line.

Fire will be maintained on the S.O.S. Line until it becomes evident that, owing to the advance made by the enemy, fire at close ranges is necessary in order to protect the Reserve Line.

Fire on the S.O.S. Line, in conjunction with that of the Artillery and Trench Mortars, should prevent the enemy being reinforced, and thus enable the Infantry garrison and Forward Machine Guns to deal effectively with those enemy troops who may have succeeded in penetrating the front position.

28.—S.O.S. SIGNAL.

It will rarely be possible for the Rear Guns to have their fire controlled by direct observation from the vicinity of the gun position. Communication by runner is obviously out of the question, being far too slow for S.O.S. purposes. Visual signalling and telephonic communications are the only alternatives. The normal method of signalling an attack is the sending up by the Infantry of a S.O.S. Signal. This is effective provided it is observed, but it is a common experience that the S.O.S. Signal is either missed or misunderstood. The Machine Guns cannot afford to wait until they hear the Artillery opening up ; for it is the *rôle* of the Rear Machine Guns to open fire on their S.O.S. Line the moment the attack is signalled, and, if possible, before the enemy have reached our wire. The greatest value of these guns is during the first two minutes of an attack, and they must aim to get their fire down even more speedily than the Artillery, and even before the Very lights have burnt out.

It is therefore necessary that all Machine Gunners should know what the Signal is, from where it will be fired, and in what direction. Picking up the S.O.S. Signal should be frequently rehearsed both on Field Ranges and in the line. If there is any risk that the S.O.S. Signal will not be picked up by the Rear Guns, a Forward Observation Officer, connected with these by telephone, should be stationed in front. There are numerous examples of the successful results of such an arrangement.

29.—TELEPHONIC COMMUNICATION.

1. No proper system of Fire Control is possible without telephonic communication. This is indispensable between : —

(*a*) Forward Observation Posts and : —

       (i.) O.C. Machine Guns in the Brigade Area.

       (ii.) Rear Guns.

       (iii.) Report Centres of Forward Guns.

(*b*) O.C. Machine Guns in the Brigade Area and:—

       (i.) Rear Guns.

       (ii.) Report Centres of Forward Guns.

(*c*) Divisional Machine Gun Commander and O.C. Machine Guns in the several Brigade Areas.

2. In addition, every effort should be made to link up by telephone, pairs of Forward Guns with their Report Centres, of which there should be two or more in each Brigade Area connected up with the Forward Observation Post and the O.C. Machine Guns in the manner just described.

Wherever possible telephone communication must be duplicated by visual signalling.

The Report Centre will usually be a Battalion Headquarters (*see* Sec. 4, para. 12), and, therefore, when separate lines are not available, it should be possible to arrange that the Forward Guns can send and receive messages from the Headquarters of the nearest Infantry Company over the Battalion line.

3. Communication with the rear *viâ* the Divisional Machine Gun Commander puts the guns in immediate touch with information from the Artillery, the Royal Flying Corps and adjacent Divisions.

4. It is only by the above means that it will be possible to make the Machine Gun defence flexible, rapid in execution, and of the greatest value to Infantry Battalions.

30.—THE BATTERY SYSTEM.

1. The Battery System, *i.e.*, a group of guns usually eight in number under the control of a Battery Commander, is an established feature of barrage work in offensive operations. The system can be applied to the defensive barrage. It is possible that here a battery of four guns, which is less easy of detection, may be a large enough unit in normal conditions, but the better the communications the more elastic the Battery system can become, without sacrificing its fundamental characteristic—unity of control.

2. An arrangement of the Main Line Defence on the Battery principle has these advantages:—

(*a*) It suits the principle of defence in depth.

(*b*) It saves much time which is otherwise spent in the tour and inspection of isolated gun positions.

(*c*) It reduces to a minimum the difficulties of ammunition supply.

(*d*) It makes the system of defence more flexible. The Rear Guns will be available for other work than fire on a single S.O.S. Line. Their fire can be switched on to new danger zones, in response to calls from the Divisional Machine Gun Commander, Forward Observation Officer and Infantry Commanders. The speedy response of the concentrated fire of many guns is the most telling fashion in which the surprise effect of Machine Guns can in existing conditions be attained.

(*e*) It makes the Machine Guns a better instrument for co-operation with the Artillery in the " offensive " defence.

3. A combination consisting of the minimum of Forward Guns, consistent with their being able to perform the duties already outlined, and of Rear Guns organized on the Battery system, will be found a good working combination under most circumstances, especially when the defence is that of newly won ground, where little or no protection for Forward Guns exists.

31.—SNIPING BATTERIES.

A Battery connected by telephone with a forward observation station can be employed as a Sniping Battery. By the aid of his Fighting Map (*see* Part II.) the Forward Observation Officer is able to send down the necessary fire orders in a simple form in the minimum of time. On many parts of the front visible targets are rare, but after a successful offensive they are often numerous, and where Sniping Batteries have been employed on the principles laid down in this publication they have obtained good results.

Trained observation is indispensable. The observer who is conversant with the principles of the enemy's scheme of defence (*see* Sec. 39), will be able to locate targets from momentary glimpses and casual hints which would be lost on the uninformed observer, however keen his eyesight.

The reporting of targets, and of fire effect (when this can be observed), gives confidence to the Machine Gun personnel, and at a minimum cost in material stops overland movement by day within Machine Gun range.

32.—SITING OF MACHINE GUNS.

1. Guns must be sited with reference to the *rôle* they have to play in the plan of defence. One of the disadvantages of putting guns in the vicinity of the Front Line is that the gun position is subject to continuous enemy annoyance and supervision, and to complete destruction in case of an intense enemy bombardment. The position is, therefore, likely to be weak tactically and materially. A site, well in rear of the Front Line, can be selected in the strongest tactical position, and the strong points or trench lines can be planned to conform to the lines of fire of the Machine Guns.

2. In general, owing to the concentrated Artillery fire which is likely to be directed on it, positions in any clearly defined trench system should be avoided. Aerial observation, however, makes the concealment of positions in the open increasingly difficult. Such a position should not be surrounded by belts of high wire, which indicate its presence to the airman. During the process of construction, the excavation and building materials should be carefully camouflaged. Even though all movement takes place at night, tracks may be made which show up on photographs. It is, therefore, often advisable to select a site near a piece of trench system and use this as an avenue of approach. The track from the trench to the position can then be continued past the position to a trench beyond it, and made to resemble a new short cut in the existing trench system.

3. Mobility, alternative positions, and frequent changes of location are, along with camouflage, the best ways of ensuring concealment. The further the guns are from the

35

Front Line, the less the difficulties of moving. A change of location will be imperative for a Battery of guns, if there are clear indications that they have been spotted.

4. Wire entanglements should be arranged so as to force the enemy in a particular direction, which will bring him into a belt of Machine Gun fire.

It is not advisable to place Machine Guns in the angle of the wire, where the enemy is bound to suspect their presence. Only dummy emplacements should be constructed at these points, the actual Machine Gun emplacements being sited in concealed ground to a flank or in rear.

In the laying out of new Field Works and new wire, close co-operation between the Engineers and the Machine Gun Corps is essential. (*See* Sec. 17, para. 3; and Sec. 36, para. 5.)

6. (*a*) The slope of the ground is an important consideration in the siting of Machine Guns; and for the Machine Gunners the choice of slope will usually be wide when the scheme of defence is in depth and the ground is surveyed from the standpoint of the Division and Corps.

(*b*) A forward slope offers the big advantage of direct laying and continuous observation of the movements of troops, in case the guns have to change from long range indirect fire to direct fire across their immediate front. The serious drawback is the risk of detection from enemy observation posts or balloons, and the difficulty of moving while under observation. Where the position on the forward slope can be ingeniously concealed, it may, by its inherent improbability, escape artillery fire.

(*c*) A reverse slope now presents no serious drawback to overhead fire. Its advantage is that it allows of unobserved movement up to the position. When guns are in a Battery, it also conceals the unavoidable traffic between gun and gun, but because of its natural advantages it is likely to be marked down by the enemy's artillery, and (if it is an isolated feature) to be subjected to a concentration of fire.

(*d*) The ideal slope is, perhaps, one defiladed from the front and sloping obliquely to the enemy. This kind of slope is more likely to offer itself in hilly country with spurs and intersecting valleys. The guns can then be sited so that they flank any attempt to cross the valley and, with frontal fire, prevent the enemy ascending it. Care must be taken in these cases that the tops of the ridges are commanded by guns placed in other positions.

33.—TYPES OF EMPLACEMENT.

1. The type of emplacement selected will be governed by the *rôle* of the gun, the lie of the ground, the labour available, the nature of the soil and the proximity of the enemy.

2. *Covered Loophole Emplacements.*—These, when built into a clearly defined trench system (as contrasted with strongholds in woods and industrial areas), are seldom suitable nowadays. Even strong concrete will not stand a modern bombardment, and the loophole faces get knocked about or blocked up or masked by shell debris. In sandy ground there is an additional drawback: unless the floor of the loophole emplacement is made of solid material and kept swept of sand hourly, the draught, when the loophole screen is lowered, drives a cloud of sand on to the gun and into the firer's face. Furthermore, the cordite fumes from certain marks of S.A.A. are injurious to the gun numbers confined in such an emplacement, and will necessitate the wearing of respirators during firing. On the other hand, firing under cover, in addition to reducing minor casualties, increases the gunner's confidence.

Covered emplacements will often be found suitable:—

(*a*) In naturally protected places such as woods, houses and mine buildings.

(*b*) In battery positions, when these are sited on reverse slopes, from which the work of construction will not be visible to the enemy. In this case there will be no loopholes. (*See* diagram in Appendix II.)

3. *Open emplacements*, connected by covered way or open trench, with neighbouring emplacements and a central dug-out.

The advantage of this type is that it is easily constructed, so that numerous alternative positions can be. prepared in advance. In Battery positions the open emplacement facilitates fire control, setting out of aiming posts, and laying off from reference objects. If, however, the central dug-out is any distance from the emplacements, there is a danger that the team will never reach them under a bombardment.

The most modern form of open emplacement is the adapted shell hole, or series of shell-holes, which from its resemblance to the surrounding terrain is difficult to detect.

4. *Emplacements of the Champagne Type.*—The plan is a double shaft leading up from a dug-out between the two. One shaft is the entrance, and from the other shaft the gun is fired.

There is, therefore, no distance between the dug-out and the gun position. The firing shaft opens out into a shell-hole, or bit of natural cover, or on to a carefully camouflaged slit in the ground. In isolated positions, or positions covering strong points, this is generally the best type of emplacement.

A strong tunnelled system leading out to inconspicuous emplacements, which are little more than stances for the gun, combines many of the advantages of covered and open emplacements. Weak tunnels, however, are only traps.

34.—EQUIPMENT OF GUN POSITIONS.

1. Whether in actual occupation or not, all gun positions, other than alternative positions, should be equiped with the following:—

(i.) Order Board.   } *See* Appendix I.
(ii.) List of Stores. }
(iii.) Fighting Map.

Occupied positions only :—

Intelligence Summary.

2. The Fighting Maps should show the Zero line, line of fire for S.O.S., line of fire for close defence, and the lines of fire of the guns on either flank.

The Intelligence Summary should contain:—

(i.) The calculations from which the Fighting Map has been made.

(ii.) List of targets (with calculations) for harassing fire.

(iii.) A record of all fighting done and the targets engaged.

(iv.) Notes on the ground visible from the gun position.

(v.) Position of Section Officer's Dug-out, and the Machine Gun Company Headquarters.

(vi.) Information as to relief routes, dumps, etc.

3. Wherever possible gun positions should be provided with a shelter for belt filling and gun cleaning, and also with a dug-out for the gun team. Recesses should be constructed in which to keep the gun, spare parts, and belt boxes. One of these recesses should be made gas proof, and at least half the belt boxes at the gun kept in it.

CHAPTER IV.

85.—ATTACK AND DEFENCE OF WOODED AREAS AND TOWNS.

1. *Wooded Areas.*—Large wooded areas will be the scene of highly organized resistance, owing to the fact that they lend themselves to defence by nests of Machine Guns, distributed in depth. The attacking troops can be diverted by well arranged obstacles, natural and artificial (thickets, wire, palissades, and the like), on to paths or clearings which are swept by the fire of concealed Machine Guns. Even when the gun has been located, it will be hard to silence, for it will be in a strong position, fortified with loopholes and overhead protection, which is denied to Artillery observation by the surrounding undergrowth and foliage.

If such an area has to be attacked, it can only be reduced by the systematic process of a piecemeal bombardment. Its reduction will be of necessity very slow, and the individual Machine Gun will not be handicapped by its environment. The Artillery can only single out for special concentration a particular part of a forest, in the sense that they can single out a particular map square in any area of similar dimensions.

2. *Towns and Industrial Areas.*—(a) Such areas cannot be passed by or easily enveloped like a small village. Envelopment will usually be the aim of the attacking force, but when the process involves a Corps or a whole Army, the Brigades and Divisions in the heart of it will be compelled to fight for the ground in detail and incorporate the pieces, as they are won, into a scheme of suburban defences.

(b) To erect a protective belt either by direct bands of fire or obliquely locked zones (*see* Sec. 14), is a difficult thing in a maze of half-demolished buildings; but a big town, with a central area and suburbs and streets leading out to these across a waste of fields, railway sidings, reservoirs, slag heaps, and the like, offers exceptional opportunities for a defensive flanking barrage.

(c) The same holds good for the attack. Such a district is reduced irregularly in the process of envelopment. Unusual salients are created by the artificial features on the ground. It is, therefore, generally possible to obtain positions from which the streets, in whatever direction they run, can be caught in enfilade.

(*d*) A " set-piece " attack will therefore tend to take the following form:—Whilst the Heavy Artillery bombards the mine heads (Fosses, Puits, etc.), public buildings, chateaux, and street rows, the Machine Guns will supplement the barrage of the Field Artillery by placing a flanking barrage along slag heaps, avenues and streets. The occupants of the houses, if they try to run away, will (in the absence of underground communications) either be caught by Machine Gun fire, or confined to the tedious and dangerous course of working from ruin to ruin. All traffic junctions within range and strike of the bullet (the two things are by no means identical) will be similarly swept.

(*e*) Frontal fire on roofs and walls is very demoralising to the occupants. It will, therefore, be advisable to combine frontal with enfilade fire.

As this kind of frontal fire is mainly for moral effect, each gun can be given a bigger frontage than usual, and this will free more guns for the enfilade of different streets.

(*f*) A rain of harassing fire at night, planned on the same principles, and incessantly maintained, will greatly lower the spirit of the defence.

(*g*) When Machine Guns are placed among buildings, Reference Objects are usually very hard to find. Often nothing can be seen from the position except the immediate field of fire, so that the gun must be laid for indirect fire by compass.

(*h*) As a site for Machine Guns, a house is to be avoided if it is isolated or if it abuts on cross roads, but when it forms part of a group it offers certain advantages:—

(i.) The cellars make dry and comfortable dugouts; and when they have been in enemy occupation, many will already have been strengthened. In this case, however, precautions must be taken against traps and land mines. The ventilation holes facing the enemy must be strongly covered; and, when captured buildings are first entered, it must be remembered that it is the enemy's custom to block up the front windows and leave gaps or open windows in the rear, through which the light of a match or torch will be detected.

(ii.) Provided that it has been strutted (which usually is feasible owing to the abundance of mine props and derelict wood-work), the basement of a house will sometimes withstand a direct hit on the house itself. In that case the growing pile of bricks adds to the strength of the cellars beneath.*

(iii.) Cellar windows afford natural loopholes in abundance, and require little or no external work before use as a Machine Gun emplacement. If they become masked by shell debris it is usually possible to find an alternative position outside without much difficulty. Whether the emplacement is inside or outside the cellar, care will have to be taken that the gun and ammunition boxes are kept clear of brick dust, which, mixing with the oil, forms a paste that clogs the working parts of the gun.

(iv.) Where the upper storeys are standing, they are useful as observation posts; and on occasions Machine Guns can be fired from them. Instances have occurred in which Machine Guns so placed have covered the advance of Infantry with direct overhead fire, sweeping the top of the Fosse or other point, which was the Infantry's objective.

---

* The enemy makes a practice of building concrete emplacements in a ground floor room, and firing his Machine Guns through the window or a hole. These emplacements are a room within a room, and apparently capable of withstanding the heaviest shelling.

CHAPTER V.

36.—ORGANIZATION OF DEFENCE OF CAPTURED POSITIONS.

1. The principles of organizing in depth the defence of ground won are identical with those that govern the placing of Machine Guns in a system of highly organized defences.

2. The Forward Guns, whose *rôle* during the offensive has been detailed in Sec. 4, will be sited with a view to carrying out the same duties in defence. As they move up to their selected positions in the manner already described (Sec. 4, paras. 5-9), these guns, in conjunction with the Rear Guns following on behind, will at no stage violate the principle of a distribution in depth, and from the outset of their location in a new environment will assume naturally a *rôle* similar to that which they discharged in the settled warfare of the trenches.

3. In the plan drafted before the opening of the offensive operation, the problem of disposing Machine Guns in depth will need to be considered as a whole, and the disposition taken will conform to the arrangements then made.

4. These arrangements will contemplate a scheme of defence of the same order as before (*see* Sec. 13), namely:—

    (*a*) A series of defended shell-holes, etc., not forming a continuous line, corresponding to the First Line in ordinary trench warfare.

    (*b*) A line of supporting points, corresponding to the Support Line, and occupied in greater depth.

    (*c*) A line of defended localities, or converted enemy entrenchments, corresponding to the Reserve Line.

5. The reconnaissance for the Forward Guns should be made in conjunction with the reconnoitring detachment of Engineers, which follows in the wake of the attacking Infantry. When the gun teams reach their destination, their function will be two-fold:—

    (i.) To cover Infantry and Working Parties of Pioneers who are engaged on the construction of strong points and lines of resistance.

(ii.) To co-operate with the Engineers in laying out Machine Gun fields of fire and constructing Machine Gun emplacements, the object being to secure a sequence of work, in which, as the initial stage, Machine Gun fields of fire are selected with reference to the possibilities of the ground, and themselves determine the conformation of the wire which the Engineers are proceeding to lay.

When the organization of the defence is sufficiently advanced, the guns will, where necessary, move from the positions temporarily taken up in the course of the battle to those allotted to them in the newly constructed system in accordance with the plans of the Commander (*see* Section 17, para. 3).

6. The Forward Guns will be located normally between the Support and Reserve Lines. As in the defence of highly organized positions, they will have two lines of fire :—

(*a*) Between the advanced posts of the Front Line on to the ground in front, which they will protect with a belt of Type " B " (as described in Sec. 14 and Sec. 21, para. 3).

(*b*) Along the ground in front of the Support Line, which they will protect with bands of short range fire.

As the advanced posts do not form a continuous line, their power of resistance will be strengthened, without risk to the occupants, by Machine Guns firing between them from the rear.

7. The forward movement of the Rear Guns (*see* Sec. 10), demands judicious timing and foresight.

(*a*) From the nature of their employment they cannot cross No Man's Land before the enemy barrage comes down. Some time after Zero, they must pass through this barrage, thick or thin. Therefore, as much latitude as possible should be allowed to them as regards the moment at which they will move forward.

(*b*) The fire of the Rear Guns at their intermediate positions is an essential part of the battle action, and either from there, or from their final positions, they will nearly always be called upon for a S.O.S. barrage. Every effort should therefore be made to avoid selecting positions on the enemy's barrage line. The fact that the enemy will naturally select for his barrage distinctive lines like a support trench. a road or a river, must be set against the temptation to send the Rear Guns to these easily recognisable features. If the Rear Guns have the misfortune to strike the barrage line, their fire may be neutralized, and they may be forced to move elsewhere. This will involve the working out of new calculations, which is a difficult matter in the stress of an action, even for a highly trained personnel.

(c) The Divisional Machine Gun Commander must carefully lay down beforehand the organization of the Rear Guns after an attack. Even when the Battery System is maintained as a normal part of the defensive structure, certain modifications in detail (re-grouping, thinning out of Batteries, etc.) will usually be necessary.

(d) Owing to the strain, physical and nervous, which is imposed on a team that has first of all to fire a timed barrage, and subsequently to keep on the alert for S.O.S. calls, their relief should not be delayed, preparations having been made for this in advance in accordance with Sec. 6, para. 3. When fresh Divisions take over the new line, they will be apt to press for the retention of the old personnel, who are familiar with the situation. But all experience is against the policy of keeping the same teams in the same barrage positions longer than is absolutely necessary after the attack.

(e) The plan of defence will be completed by the final location of the Rear Guns in rear of the new Reserve Line. There they will resume a defensive *rôle*, two-fold in nature, corresponding to that which they occupied before the advance. (*See* Sec. 23, para. 2.)

CHAPTER VI.

WARFARE OF IMPROVISED DEFENCES AND OPEN FIGHTING.

37.—SPECIAL CONSIDERATIONS.

1. Important as are the organization and arrangement of the work of Machine Guns in warfare against highly organized defences, they are even more important after the main defended area has been broken through, and the fighting has resolved itself into the attack and defence of more or less hastily organized defences.

2. The more open the fighting becomes, the more will troops get away from the " mass " of their artillery and have to depend on Machine Guns to do some portion of the work for which they have been accustomed to rely on the Artillery.

It is precisely in places where such a situation arises that a working scheme between the Artillery, Machine Guns, and Trench Mortars will enable a division of labour to be arranged, in which, by taking on definite tasks, such as the neutralization of certain areas, the Machine Guns will be able to do some of the Artillery work, and thereby enable the Artillery to concentrate more guns for other and perhaps more important purposes.

3. The more open the fighting, the more effective is the Machine Gun, and the more self-reliance and judgment are required to apply the principles laid down in this publication: and if (to take an extreme case) the Artillery were entirely eliminated, the Machine Gun would be called upon to provide the principal neutralizing and covering fire.

In trench warfare the Artillery is the principal protection of the Infantry against enemy Machine Guns. While the enemy are in occupation of a highly organized defensive area, which has been under close observation for a long period, it is more difficult for the enemy to conceal the position of his Machine Guns, and, therefore, easier for the Artillery to destroy them, or at any rate neutralize their fire.

But in more open conditions of fighting it will be much harder for the Artillery to locate and deal with them.

Furthermore, whenever the enemy resistance is stout, the advance must be preceded and supported by some form of covering fire. Open warfare implies movement. The Machine Gun is more mobile than the Field Gun, and it is the only weapon outside the Artillery which is capable of covering an attack by sustained long range overhead fire.

4. Care must be taken to ensure that in the confusing circumstances of a considerable forward movement, the fire power of the Machine Guns is not misapplied or wasted. Machine Guns at once lose the greater part of their value if they are hurried forward from their limbers, with inadequate supplies of ammunition, into positions where their fire is masked by Lewis Guns and Infantry outposts. The comparative mobility of the Machine Guns does not mean that their teams on foot can keep pace with a Battalion. Similarly, though Machine Guns on pack animals can go wherever a horse can go, when removed from pack animals they are less mobile than Cavalry units.

The definite attachment of Machine Guns to Infantry Battalions (*see* Sec. 4, para. 2) generally defeats its own end. Machine Guns, if they are kept well in hand, are at once an instrument of offence and a reserve of fire power within reach of the Infantry Commander; but, if they are involved in the details of a Battalion's movements, full use cannot be made of them.

5. · The situation which has to be foreseen is one in which little or no Artillery is for the moment available. Machine Guns will be called upon, and, if properly handled, should be able to assist in making good the shortage of Artillery. Apart from their obvious value for strengthening the covering fire, the effective use of Machine Guns for neutralizing strong points, nests of Machine Guns, and even the Field Battery positions of the enemy—tasks which in the conditions of warfare hitherto prevailing have been relegated almost entirely to the Artillery—may make the whole difference between the success or failure of operations in which the available Artillery support is necessarily limited.

6. This, however, pre-supposes :—

(*a*) A high standard of training and technical ability on the part of Machine Gunners.

(*b*) The allotment of suitable tasks in advance and careful arrangements to that end.

(*c*) The closest co-operation with the Artillery.

Co-operation with the Artillery in trench warfare, and in the preparation for and execution of " set piece " offensives, is the best guarantee that these *desiderata* will be forthcoming later.

38.—GENERAL PRINCIPLES.

1. The general principles for the employment of Machine Guns are the same, whether the warfare be that of highly organized defences, or warfare of a more open nature. While the enemy is himself on the move, the fire power of Machine Guns must be used to endeavour to prevent him settling down, but once he has taken up a defensive position, a " set-piece " attack has usually to be organized, and then, however small the attack may be, the work of the available Machine Guns must be prepared in exactly the same manner as has already been described.

2. However open the warfare may become, the organization of the Machine Guns still falls naturally into two distinct categories:—

> (*a*) The guns pushed forward to support closely the Infantry Battalions and corresponding to the Forward Guns, whose duties have been described in Secs. 4 and 36.

> (*b*) The guns retained for special covering fire, either direct or indirect, and corresponding to the Rear Guns. (*See* Secs. 5 and 36.)

3. (*a*) If the Machine Guns are to be of real assistance to the attacking troops when the available 18-pdr. support is limited, a high percentage of the total guns must be detailed for the duty mentioned in para. 2 (*b*) above.

Otherwise it will be impossible to re-concentrate the Machine Guns for overhead covering fire, either for assisting the Infantry advance, or resisting counter-attacks against positions already gained.

(*b*) The Machine Guns allotted under para. 2 (*b*) above should:—

> (i.) Be organized in Mobile Batteries of 4, 6, or 8 guns each, as convenient.

> (ii.) Advance by bounds and be allotted definite halting places at the end of each bound.

> (iii.) Keep in close touch with the advancing Infantry, so as to be able to move up quickly and come into action when and where required.

(*c*) Each Group of Mobile Batteries should be under the command of an officer detailed as Group Commander.

This officer must make a careful study of the ground on his probable route of advance, consider the various positions from which he may be called upon to use his Batteries, and have his Headquarters at the Headquarters of the Brigade whose advance he is covering.

(*d*) In the event of a complete initial success, formations pushing forward early beyond the range of adequate Field Artillery support should be allotted a large proportion of the available Mobile Batteries in order that the shortage of Field Artillery may in some measure be made good.

(*e*) Machine Guns pushed forward " amongst " the Infantry are seldom able to render actual support during an advance, and are mainly of use for the defence of the ground won. These guns should therefore : —

    (i.) Be only a small proportion of the total number available.

    (ii.) Usually work in sub-sections.

    (iii.) Advance by bounds along a definite line of advance.

    (iv.) Be allotted definite halting places at the end of each bound.

(*f*) The organization of a large proportion of the available Machine Guns into Mobile Batteries, has, in addition to its power of offensive action by supporting the Infantry advance, the great advantage of : —

    (i.) Forming a strong rear line of defence in case of a reverse.

    (ii.) Forming a reserve of fire power in the hand of the Commander, available to assist in exploiting a success.

(*g*) The question of the supply of an adequate amount of S.A.A. for the Mobile Batteries is necessarily a difficult one, and all arrangements for getting it forward and the forming of advanced dumps must be carefully worked out before the advance begins.

(*h*) For the organization of the defence the fire power of Machine Guns is best employed by having a small proportion of the available Machine Guns forward for defence *in depth* of the ground gained, and the remainder retained in their battery organization for the purpose of : —

    (i.) Putting down an S.O.S. barrage along the front of the position to be defended.

    (ii.) Concentrating their fire against a counter-attack, or on an area from which a counter-attack is being initiated.

(*i*) The placing of large numbers of Machine Guns actually *in* the position to be defended has proved itself to be wasteful in personnel and material, and not nearly so effective as the method outlined in (*h*) above.

(*j*) The Divisional Machine Gun Commander should not personally command a group of Machine Gun Batteries.

He should keep in close touch with his Divisional Head-quarters, supervise generally the supply arrangements of the forward Batteries, and be in readiness to direct any reorganization necessary to meet a change of circumstances.

4. In regions where the enemy makes a voluntary retirement to conform with a retirement imposed on him elsewhere, we shall have to pass through, and perhaps remain on, a network of undestroyed fortifications. The Machine Guns will have to be placed either in these fortifications or in the vacant ground between them. In these circumstances the following considerations must be weighed:—

(*a*) An old strong point may only have been a strong point because it contained guns and faced a certain way. It will be known to the enemy, and if it possesses no natural strength it should be avoided.

(*b*) In winter especially, it will be of convenience to select positions near to existing dug-outs which are water proof and perhaps shell proof. The fact that prepared defences need a minimum of new work is an argument in their favour.

5. In organized defences the task of silencing enemy Machine Guns belongs primarily to the Artillery, but among improvised defences Machine Guns will be capable of taking a bigger share in this. Lewis Guns, owing to their greater mobility, will be more successful in stalking single Machine Guns at close quarters, but Machine Guns should be effective in silencing by concentrated fire active enemy nests.

6. In warfare of an open nature there will be full scope for the bold handling of Machine Guns, but boldness does not mean unnecessary exposure to Artillery fire or snipers.

7. Machine Guns will in most cases be sufficiently protected by the dispositions of the troops with whom they are acting. Where the Machine Gun Commander finds himself in an exposed position, he will take such steps as may be necessary to guard his detachment against surprise.

8. The situation will sometimes arise in which the simultaneous delivery of two or more loosely connected attacks results in exposing the inner flanks of the attacking forces. Should an attack develop against a line of defended localities, it may happen that neighbouring troops are drawn apart towards the several centres of resistance, thus creating a gap through which the enemy can issue to deliver a counter attack on their flanks.

A battery of Machine Guns, placed so as to command the ground over which the counter attack is likely to come, will be able, owing to the great fire power which it can instantly develop, to nip in the bud any such enterprise on the part of the enemy. The method of controlling the fire of Machine Gun Batteries, described in Part II. of this publication, enables their fire to be directed rapidly on to a new target or threatened area.

39.—RECONNAISSANCE AND APPRECIATION OF THE TACTICAL SITUATION.

1. An accurate knowledge of the enemy's method of defence is desirable, inasmuch as the enemy is himself expert in Machine Gun defence, and takes the weight of our assault on a zone of defences cleverly studded with Machine Guns. Moreover, as territory is gradually wrested from him, it becomes necessary to incorporate into our own defended system, ground that has already been put in a state of defence by him. Machine Gun Officers should, therefore, study carefully the Intelligence Summaries and special publications in which the information on this subject, obtained from prisoners and captured orders, is reproduced.

2. This general knowledge must be supplemented by exact reconnaissance on the ground itself. A study of the map and, through glasses, of the ground in combination with the map must precede and follow the actual visit to the ground This will make the reconnaissance what it should be—the recognition of a situation already envisaged in the rough. The picture thus obtained should be checked, when occasion offers, by aerial photographs, and the map kept up to date by the insertion of new details extracted from the Intelligence Summaries. None of these aids, however, should be allowed to interfere with the examination of the actual ground.

In the isolated operations of more open warfare, Machine Gun Officers will have to collect for themselves much of the information which is supplied by Army Headquarters on the eve of a " set-piece " offensive. Only thus will it be possible to select in advance suitable localities for the guns and to detect places from which trouble is likely to occur.

It must be remembered that the unexpected will often occur, and can only be met correctly by an intelligent application of principles.

3. The approach to positions must be conducted on the same principle as the forward movement of the Forward Guns in a " set-piece " offensive : —

> (a) The guns will keep in sub-sections of two guns at least.

> (b) From the moment of leaving limbers they will advance by " bounds."

> (c) The line of advance for the guns and their halting place at each " bound " will be laid down.

> (d) A reconnoitring officer, covered by his scouts, will go forward to reconnoitre routes, and will order up the guns to selected localities, from which they can best assist the Infantry Battalions when their assistance is required.

> (e) After the forward representative has selected the site for the guns and sent or signalled back to them, he will make arrangements to enable them to come into action as soon after their arrival as possible. He will select targets, take ranges, and make any necessary calculations. He will therefore be accompanied by his range-taker.

4. When, after a period of movement, the situation again threatens to become stationary, every officer should make a detailed reconnaissance of the area round his guns, with a view to laying the foundation of a sound scheme of defence. Too often guns are found in places which were originally intended as halting places only, or in places to which they were forced in the exigencies of an action, to the neglect of better sites in the vicinity. If sub-section and section officers after local reconnaissance send in sketches, showing alternative positions and their fields of fire, on tracing paper of the same scale as the map in use, the Commanding Officers of Companies and the Divisional Machine Gun Commander will have at all times the raw materials of a good defensive scheme.

For Cavalry, *see* " Cavalry Training," Secs. 231-3.

40.—ATTACKS ON WOODS, VILLAGES, AND OTHER DEFENDED LOCALITIES.

1. The situation under consideration in this Section is that of any army retiring on a wide front and using the woods and villages which lie on its path as rear-guard positions, from which to arrest temporarily the progress of the pursuing forces. The object of the pursuer will be to expel the enemy from its defended localities with as little delay as possible, and drive his rear guards back on his main force, before that force has had time to settle down in a prepared system or to organize new defences of an elaborate nature

2. (a) Whenever these defended localities are sufficiently adjacent to each other they will undoubtedly be organised for mutual support by the long range fire of Artillery and Machine Guns.

(b) An operation against such a line will accordingly take the form, either of a simultaneous attack against the line on a wide front, or of attacks on certain localities to attract the enemy's attention, hold him to the ground, and wear down his power of resistance in combination with attacks on other localities, the capture of which will make it possible to envelop the enemy on either flank and cut off the retreat of his garrisons. (F.S.R., Sec. 103.)

The latter form of operation will, at the same time, probably allow a portion of the force which has broken through to push on rapidly and disorganize the retirement of the enemy's main body.

3. (a) As a rule, therefore, envelopment will be the preferable method; and the enveloping movements of the Infantry will be covered by the fire of Machine Guns from the front and flanks of the locality which is being surrounded. For this purpose a large number of the available guns will be employed with advantage for long range covering and searching fire, either direct or indirect.

(b) As the enveloping movements of the Infantry progress, Machine Guns will be moved to suitable positions on the flanks of the locality, from which enfilade and oblique fire can be brought against the flanks and rear of the defences.

(c) Long range fire from Machine Guns can also be used to cover the exits from the locality, thus preventing reinforcements and barring the lines of retreat to the defenders.

Fire of this kind will lower the morale of the defenders by producing that feeling of insecurity which always arises from a knowledge that the lines of retirement are under fire.

(d) In the case of villages, doors, windows, roofs, backs of houses, streets—especially those running at right angles to the attack—should be subject to the searching fire of Machine Guns.

(e) When the attacking troops have made good the edge, or some portion of the locality, some of the Forward Machine Guns may be brought up for their closer support. At the same time the fire power of these guns must not be wasted by placing them in positions where they are liable to be masked by our own troops, or in which Lewis Guns, owing to their portability, can do equal, if not better, work. The general rule will be that Lewis Guns are used in the more advanced positions, and the Machine Guns kept in the positions further back, where they can be best used to give supporting fire.

41.—DEFENCE OF WOODS, VILLAGES, AND OTHER DEFENDED LOCALITIES.

1. *Woods.*—(a) Isolated clumps are always to be avoided, as they invite concentrated artillery fire, but clusters of woods and woods of medium size, even though they are not part of a highly organized forest system, offer natural advantages for hiding Machine Guns. It is a long time before the trees are reduced to leafless sticks which afford no cover from view. Furthermore, trees stumps and undergrowth are ideal objects in which to fasten and hide wire.

(b) As, however, woods will always be subjected to more or less heavy shelling, the minimum of men should be retained to garrison them. This entails the plan being drawn up chiefly with a view to defence by Machine and Lewis Guns, covered by forward posts of Riflemen and Bombers. Through the smallness of their numbers the defenders will have plenty of elbow room, and thus be able to shift their positions and avoid those parts of the wood which are subjected to the heaviest shelling.

(c) In basing the scheme of defence on the fire of Machine and Lewis Guns, it must not be forgotten that while these weapons can deal with any attack which is above ground and visible, they are vulnerable to attacks by small parties, who, advancing unseen by covered approaches, penetrate into the position, and snipe or bomb the gunners at close range. In the daytime the defence can safely be left to the Machine and Lewis Guns, protected by a few posts of Riflemen and Bombers, but at night time, when it is most necessary to guard against surprise, adequate protection must be provided by Infantry Battalions.

2. *Villages.*—(*a*) The crowding of Machine Guns in villages that have not been carefully organized for defence by the construction of deep dug-outs, fortified cellars, and the like, only results in heavy loss of guns and personnel without compensating advantage.

(*b*) Positions will be sought, both in and out of the locality, from which all approaches to the village can be covered with belts of cross-fire.

(*c*) As envelopment is the most probable form of attack, Machine Guns will be posted to avoid this. Guns placed behind houses or hillocks in the outskirts of a village will often be found useful for this purpose.

(*d*) The use of houses or enclosures immediately in front of the village, which will give the enemy a commanding view of the village defences, must be denied to him.

(*e*) When Machine Guns are placed inside the village, great use can be made of a strong building as a protection against Artillery, the Machine Gun being sited behind the building and fired to a flank.

42.—OCCUPATION OF VARIOUS POSITIONS.

1. Machine Guns may be hidden in almost any position, but it is unwise to choose places which are either obvious or easy to recognize, such as cross roads or isolated objects. Guns should merge into the surroundings, and straight edges or distinct shadows should be avoided. When a position has been camouflaged, the success of the work will be best determined by reports from our own airmen.

2. Banks of rivers, canals, railways, ditches, folds in the ground, hedges, palings and walls may be used either as gun positions or as a covered avenue of approach.

3. Machine Guns in crops are difficult to detect from the same level, but unless the camouflage can be made to resemble the crops, the position will be easily picked out by enemy aircraft. A field covered with manure heaps or mounds of roots makes a better background.

4. If a barricade has been constructed across a road, Machine Guns should not be put on the barricade itself, but in a concealed position to a flank from which they can fire down the road or across and along the barricade.

5. Hay stacks and trees are more suitable for observation posts than for emplacements; but, in the same way as buildings in villages, they can be used to defilade Machine Guns which are located behind them and fire to either flank.

43.—ADVANCED GUARDS.

1. The duties of an advanced guard make it necessary that great fire power should be available when required. A large proportion of Machine Guns should therefore be allotted to advanced guards.

2. These Machine Guns should be well forward in the column, so that they may be able to get quickly into action: but if employed in support of the leading troops, they should be protected against surprise.

3. The principal duties of Machine Guns with the advanced guard are:—

> (i.) To assist in driving back enemy forces by rapid production of great fire power at the required point.

> (ii.) To assist in holding any position gained until the arrival of the main body.

> (iii.) To cover the deployment of the main body by holding the enemy on a wide front.

4. Machine Guns will normally be employed with the main guard, but with large forces it will often be of advantage to employ some Machine Guns with the vanguard. For example, with an advanced guard consisting of an Infantry Brigade, which has as much as a Battalion of Infantry acting with the vanguard, a normal distribution will be one section of Machine Guns with the vanguard, three sections with the main guard.

5. The section acting with the vanguard will be the Forward Guns mentioned in Sec. 38 para. 2 (*a*), and in the case of an attack being developed by the advanced guard, their *rôle* will be similar to that of the Forward Guns as described in Sec. 4. The three sections with the main guard

will be those mentioned in Sec. 38 para. 2 (*b*); and in case of an attack being developed by the advanced guard, their *rôle* will be similar to that of the Rear Guns as described in Sec. 5.

Whether their fire is direct or indirect, or whether a portion of them use direct fire and a portion indirect, will depend on the tactical circumstances of the particular situation, the nature of the ground, and the amount of Artillery at the disposal of the enemy.

44.—REAR GUARDS.

1. As a rear guard will usually be required to hold positions with the minimum of men, a large proportion of Machine Guns should be allotted to it.

2. Experience of war has shewn that well placed Machine Guns, supported by a few Infantry only, will frequently hold up an advance for long periods.

3. The method usually adopted by the enemy is to leave behind numerous Machine Guns, escorted by small parties of Infantry. These detachments occupy lines of defended localities in which, according to their orders, they hold out to the last, or up to a certain hour on a particular day.

4. In occupying a rear guard position with Machine Guns the same principles apply as for the defence in warfare of highly organised defences, the only difference being that, if the defences are of an improvised nature, the concealment of the guns will be of paramount importance.

5. The organization of the guns falls, as before, into two categories:—

(*a*) The Forward Guns, whose duties are generally those described in Sec. 21.

(*b*) The Rear Guns. These guns, using either direct or indirect fire, according to the circumstances, will be used to search with long range fire good approaches for hostile troops, and also to cover the withdrawal of the Forward Guns when this is necessary.

6. If it is required to fall back by stages, a portion of the Rear Guns, after having covered the withdrawal of the Forward Guns, can themselves become Forward Guns, the

Forward Guns taking up the work of the Rear Guns at some point further in rear.

In this way a continuous resistance will be offered to the hostile advance.

7. In addition to the ordinary principles of defence, the following points will be specially observed:—

(*a*) Covered lines of withdrawal will be reconnoitred.

(*b*) Limbered wagons will be close up to facilitate withdrawal, when the time for this comes. Pack transport will be found useful for the withdrawal of Forward Guns.

(*c*) Positions in rear will be chosen before the Machine Guns retire from their forward positions.

(*d*) A proportion of the Machine Guns will occupy the positions in rear, to cover the withdrawal of the Forward Guns. (*See* paras. 5 and 6.) Thus the withdrawal of the last gun can be covered.

8. A study of the foregoing considerations, in addition to the principles laid down in F.S.R., will enable Infantry Commanders to appreciate the nature of the resistance which they may expect to meet from enemy Machine Guns fighting a rearguard action in the open, and also will enable Machine Gun Commanders to deal skilfully with a situation in which a local retirement is temporarily imposed in the course of a general advance.

9. The principles outlined in Secs. 40-43 apply also to the employment of Machine Guns by Cavalry Units. *See* also Chapter VII.)

CHAPTER VII.

45.—THE TACTICAL HANDLING OF MACHINE GUN SQUADRONS.

1. The principles for the employment of Cavalry Machine Guns laid down in " Cavalry Training," Sections 225-236, hold good (with the exception of Sec. 225, Sec. 227, paras. 1 and 2; Sec. 228, para. 2, line 1; and Sec. 230, para. 4). The following Section is to be read as supplementary to, not substituted for, those Sections.

2. The general principles laid down in the foregoing chapters of this publication hold good where Cavalry are employed on foot.

3. *Co-operation.*—(i.) In order to ensure co-operation, the Machine Gun Commander must keep in the closest touch possible with the Commander of the Troops with whom he is acting. Thus, the Machine Gun Squadron Leader should ride with the Brigade Commander, and the section and sub-section leaders will keep in close touch with the Commanders of units to which they may be attached.

It is the duty of the Commander to allot a task to his Machine Gun Commander, who must be left to carry it out.

(ii.) Machine Guns must also co-operate with one another. To ensure this, the Machine Gun Squadron Commander will, both before and during an action, keep his sub-section officers fully informed of each other's orders and movements, and subordinate Machine Gun Commanders will neglect no opportunity of getting into touch with one another during the course of an action. Similarly, all Machine Gun Commanders will be responsible for gaining touch, and fighting in co-operation, with Machine Guns of other units acting on their flanks.

4. *Protection and Communication.*—The rule that the Commander of every body of troops is responsible for his own protection applies to Machine Gun Commanders. Since, however, for lack of personnel, a Machine Gun Commander is unable to detail reconnoitring and protective detachments and orderlies from the men under his command, his responsibility is limited to the duty of making a request to the Cavalry Commander under whose orders he is for such men to be attached to him as the situation demands.

5. *The Approach March.*—Owing to the necessity for careful reconnaissance and concealment and to the characteristics of the gun itself, Machine Guns take longer to come into action than Cavalry. Accordingly, the normal position of the Machine Gun unit during the approach march will be nearer the head of the column. Cavalry formations will be adhered to as far as possible, with a view to concealing the presence of Machine Guns.

6. *Distribution of Machine Guns.*—In actual fighting, a Machine Gun Squadron will rarely be employed as a unit. Machine Guns will be distributed among the units of the Brigade, the allotment of guns being governed by the following principles:—

(i.) Machine Guns will be attached to a unit only for a definite purpose.

(ii.) Generally, as many guns as possible will be kept in reserve, under the immediate control of the Brigade Commander. Once Machine Guns have been detached it is difficult to withdraw them should they be more urgently required elsewhere. Moreover, if Machine Guns are kept in hand until a definite occasion for their employment arises, the pack animals are spared much unnecessary fatigue.

(iii.) Sub-sections should not be broken up. Machine Guns are used with best effect in pairs, and a sub-section is organized with a view to its employment as a unit.

7. *Machine Guns in Action.*—(i.) In cases where ridden horses cannot approach reasonably near to gun positions, it will generally be found possible to have the gun and the first ammunition packs led up by dismounted gun numbers or pack leaders. A single horse can usually be placed under cover from view or fire, or both. This has the advantages of :—

(*a*) Sparing gun numbers unnecessary fatigue.

(*b*) Forming a mobile ammunition dump instead of a stationary one.

(ii.) When time allows and tools are available, guns will be dug in. Cover from view, however, often gives better protection than a hastily dug emplacement which may attract the enemy's attention.

(iii.) When guns are in position the Machine Gun Commander will allot targets and give general fire orders, but will not attempt to control directly the fire of one or more guns. Each detachment leader will control the fire of his own gun, while the Machine Gun Commander will remain free to watch the general situation, to make and receive reports, to maintain touch with his superior Commander and with the troops with whom he is co-operating, and to appreciate and conform to any change in the tactical situation.

APPENDIX I.

ORDERS FOR GUN POSITION No.........

1. Fire is only to be opened by order of the Gun Commander unless a sudden emergency arises, in which case the sentry will use his own initiative.

2. When relieving another gun team or sentry, the following facts will always be ascertained:—

   (a) Whether the gun has been fired during the relief,
   (b) If fired, what the target was.
   (c) If fired, the emplacement from which it was fired.
   (d) Whether any instructions have been received as to friendly patrols or wiring parties. • .

3. The sentry will always inspect the gun when taking over the position.

4. The sentry on duty must have an accurate knowledge of the targets shown on the fighting map.

5. In case of alarm, or a gas attack, the sentry will wake the gun team. .

6. The gun will be cleaned daily, and the *points before firing* gone through both morning and night. The gun must be kept free from dirt, and in the trenches may be kept wrapped up in a waterproof sheet or bag. Such a covering must not prevent the gun being mounted for action immediately.

7. Ammunition, spare parts, and anti-gas apparatus will be inspected daily.
   The Gun Commander will be responsible that all anti-gas apparatus is always in position and in order.

8. The lock spring will never be left compressed.
   With the Vickers gun it is generally sufficient to half-load and then press the thumb-piece when mounting the gun at night. In order to open fire, it is only necessary to complete the loading motion and press the thumb-piece.

9. All dug-outs, emplacements and ammunition recesses belonging to the gun position must be kept clean and in good repair.

SPECIAL ORDERS FOR THIS GUN POSITION.

1. The S.O.S. signal is_____

2. Action on S.O.S._____

3. Action if enemy penetrates our front line_____

4.

5.

6.

LIST OF STORES BELONGING TO THIS GUN POSITION

Article	Number	Remarks
Fighting Map ...		
Barrage Chart ...		
Intelligence Summary		
Mountings (pivot, box, wooden base, etc.) ...		
Mills Grenades ...		
Picks ...		
Shovels ...		
Refuse tin ...		
Sundries ...		

Date .... *Machine Gun Officer.*

APPENDIX II.

TYPES OF MACHINE GUN EMPLACEMENTS.

(a)

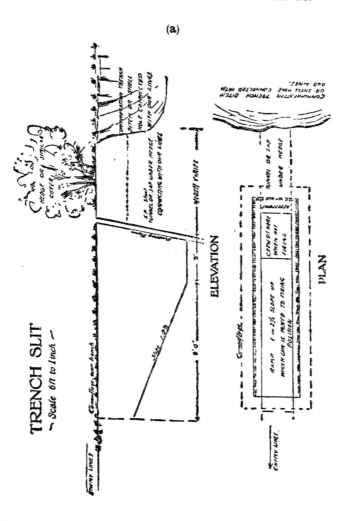

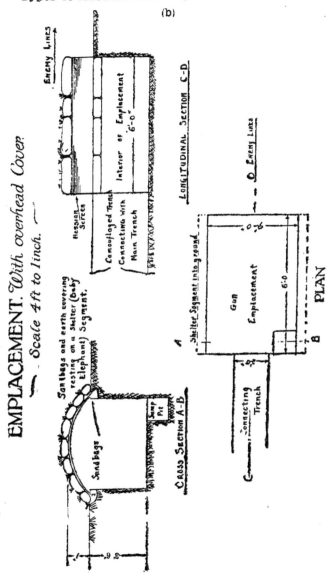

EMPLACEMENT. *With overhead Cover.*
Scale 4ft to 1inch.

LONGITUDINAL SECTION C-D

PLAN

CROSS SECTION A-B

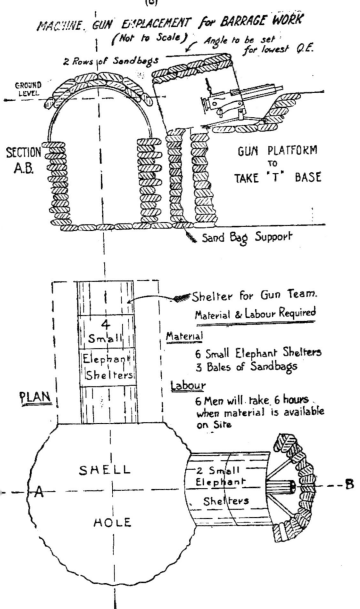

MACHINE GUN EMPLACEMENT for BARRAGE WORK
(Not to Scale) Angle to be set for lowest Q.E.

2 Rows of Sandbags

GROUND LEVEL

SECTION A.B.

GUN PLATFORM
TO
TAKE "T" BASE

Sand Bag Support

PLAN

4 Small Elephant Shelters

Shelter for Gun Team.

Material & Labour Required

Material

6 Small Elephant Shelters
3 Bales of Sandbags

Labour

6 Men will take 6 hours when material is available on Site

SHELL

A

HOLE

2 Small Elephant Shelters

B — — B

APPENDIX III.

A.—OFFENSIVE OPERATIONS.

Typical Communications of Rear Guns on a Brigade Front.

Forward Guns communicate through the Infantry Battalions in whose area they are operating.)

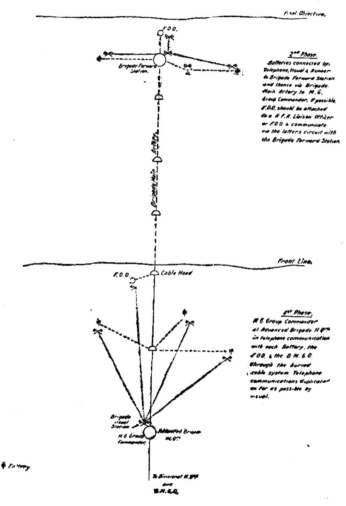

Appendix III.—*continued.*

B.—TRENCH WARFARE.

Typical Communications of Machine Guns on a Division Front.
(Forward sections communicate through the Infantry Battalions in whose area they are operating.)

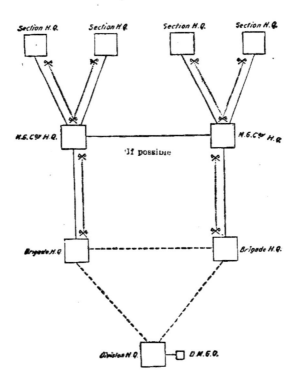

ND - #0524 - 270225 - C0 - 190/125/6 - PB - 9781908487629 - Matt Lamination